INTO AN INDIAN TENT
NATIVE AMERICAN INDIAN HOMES

US HISTORY BOOKS
CHILDREN'S AMERICAN HISTORY

BABY PROFESSOR

EDUCATION KIDS

Speedy Publishing LLC

40 E. Main St. #1156

Newark, DE 19711

www.speedypublishing.com

Copyright 2017

Native Americans built and lived in many different types of homes. The different tribes would build different homes, depending on the materials available to them as well as where they were located. Their lifestyle was taken into consideration as well as the environment. Read further to learn about these different types of homes.

LIFESTYLES OF THE NATIVE AMERICANS

Some of the tribes were known as nomads, meaning the village, in its entirety, would move from one location to another. Tribes that lived in the Great Plains often would travel like this hunting buffalo to eat. They followed the large herds of buffalo as they would roam the plains. For this reason, they built homes that were easy to build and move, known as Teepees.

Teepees

Typically, the honored seat would be facing the door and the honored guest or the man of the house would sit here.

Some of the other tribes would live in the same place for a long period of time because they had food and water nearby. They built homes that were more permanent, such as the longhouse or pueblo.

WHERE DID THE NATIVE AMERICANS LIVE?

They lived throughout North America and South America. There were Native Americans in the mainland United States, as well as Hawaii and Alaska. The different tribes would live in different areas of the country. The Plains Indians lived in the middle of the country, which included the Arapaho and Comanche tribes. The Seminole and the Cherokee tribes lived in the Southeastern United States.

Cherokee boy and girl

Wigwam

WHAT IS A WIGWAM?

The homes that were constructed by the Algonquian tribes that lived in the northeast were known as wigwams. They consisted of bark and trees, like the longhouse, however, they were easier to build and were much smaller.

Wigwam

They used the poles from trees which could be bent and tied together, making a home that was in the shape of a dome. The outside was covered with bark or any similar material

which was available and nearby. The frames
were not moveable, like that of the teepee,
but often the coverings could be transported
if the tribe moved.

The wigwam was a relatively small home, forming a circle approximately 15 feet wide. However, these homes would sometimes house more than one Native American family. It may have been a tight squeeze, however, it probably kept them warm during the winter.

There would be a flap at the top of it that was opened or closed using a pole.

Native American wigwam

Navajo hogan

WHAT IS A HOGAN?

Constructed by the Navajo peoples of the Southwest, the Hogan consisted of wooden poles used for the frame, which was covered in adobe, a clay mixed with grass. Generally, it was shaped like a dome and the door would face to the east, towards the sunrise. There was a hole at the top to enable smoke from the fire to escape.

The Hogan was often constructed with railroad ties after the 1900s.

WHAT IS A TEEPEE?

These were the houses for the Great Plains nomadic tribes. They were constructed using several long poles for the frames which were tied together at its top and spread apart at the bottom, creating an upside-down cone shaped home. The outside was then covered with a large piece of buffalo hide.

Teepees

Teepee

O nce a tribe would arrive to a new location, the women of each family would start setting up and building the teepee. They were very efficient at building the teepees, and it would typically take only 30 minutes.

Teepee

During the summer, they would raise the covering, creating a gap at the bottom of the teepee. This would enable the cool air to move throughout the teepee, keeping it cool inside.

During the winter months, they would use additional coverings and grass as insulation to keep it warm. They would build the fire in the center. In order to let the smoke out, there was a hole at the top of it.

teepee

The Plains Indians would also use the hides of buffalo for blankets and beds to keep them warm.

Typically, the teepees where the medicine men lived were decorated with paintings.

WHAT IS A NATIVE AMERICAN LONGHOUSE?

This home was constructed by the Northeast American Indians, in particular, the Iroquois nation. The Iroquois were also referred to as the Haudenosaunee, meaning "People of the Longhouses".

Iroquoian longhouse

These permanent homes were built from bark and wood and were constructed in the form of a long rectangle and were approximately 18 feet wide and 80 feet long. This is how they got their name. They had a door at each end and there would be holes in the roof allowing the smoke from the fires to escape.

To construct one of these homes, they used tall poles of trees to frame the sides in. They would use curved poles for the roof. The sides and the roof were covered with pieces of bark that overlapped, similar to shingles. This would help keep the wind and rain out.

Iroquoian village

A large village consisting of several longhouses that were built inside of a wood fence was referred to as a palisade. There would be a number of people living in a longhouse and they were known as a clan. Approximately 20 people or more would call one longhouse their home.

Palisade

Pueblo

WHAT IS A PUEBLO?

The Native American pueblo was built in the Southwest by American Indians, in particular, the Hopi tribe. These shelters were permanent and sometimes a part of bigger villages, housing hundreds, maybe thousands of people. They would often be constructed inside of caves, or sides of larger cliffs.

These homes were built using bricks consisting of adobe clay, consisting of a mixture of sand, clay, straw, and grass and then setting them to harden in the sun. Once they were hard, the bricks would be used for the wall which would then be covered with more clay to fill in the gaps. In order to keep the walls strong, each year they would place a new layer of clay on the walls.

Hopi pueblo

Hopi village

They were built of several clay rooms that were placed on top of one another. Often, they were built as tall as four or five stories. The higher the pueblo was built, the smaller the rooms would be. They used ladders to get from one floor to the other. They would then remove them at night to prevent other people from entering their house.

OTHER NATIVE AMERICAN HOMES

The plank house was built near the coast by natives located in the Northwest and were made from cedar plans. Many families lived in one home.

Plank house

Igloo

Igloos were built in Alaska by the Inuit. They were small homes shaped like domes and made of ice blocks. The igloos were able to keep the tribes warm during the cold winters. The fire inside the igloo was created by animal oil in a large dish which was used similar to a candle.

The chickee was erected by the Seminole tribes and consisted of a thatched roof which kept the rain out, however, the sides were open so they could remain cool during the Florida hot weather.

Chickee

Wattle and Daub

The wattle and daub was like the chickee, but used clay and twigs to create walls. It was constructed by tribes located in the northern, somewhat colder areas, like the North Carolina Cherokee.

TODAY'S NATIVE AMERICANS

Some descendants of the original American Indians now live on areas of land that is specifically set aside for them, known as reservations. This is to help maintain and protect their culture and heritage, even though only about 30% live on these reservations. The rest of them live just like anyone else does, outside of the reservations.

THE INDIAN RESERVATION

An area of land that is managed by a tribe under the Bureau of Indian Affairs is known as an Indian Reservation. There are 326 Indian reservations in the U.S. and each of them is associated with a Nation. Not all 526 tribes have a reservation; some tribes might have more than one, some tribes share reservations, and other may have none.

Also, due to land allotments in the past, some of the reservations are fragmented, with each piece of individual, tribal, and privately held land being considered a separate enclave. This creates significant political, legal, and administrative difficulties.

The term "reservation" stems from the idea that the Native American tribes were independent sovereigns during the time that the Constitution of the United States was ratified. Therefore, early peace treaties, which often were signed under duress, in which the Native American tribes had surrendered portions of land to the United States, also designated areas of land which the tribes reserved for themselves, and they became known as "reservations".

This term remained in place even once the government started to forcibly relocated the tribes to parcels which they had no historical connection to.

Alaskan natives

Most of the Alaska Natives and Native Americans live outside the reservations, often in large cities in the west such as Los Angeles and Phoenix. There were more than 2.5 million Native Americans in 2012, with only approximately 1 million of them living on the reservations.

Now that you have learned about the homes of the Native Americans Indians, you may have additional questions about their lives. For additional information you can go to your local library, research the internet, or ask questions of your teachers, families and friends.

Visit

BABY PROFESSOR
EDUCATION KIDS

www.BabyProfessorBooks.com

to download Free Baby Professor eBooks
and view our catalog of new and exciting
Children's Books

Made in the USA
San Bernardino, CA
27 September 2017